Can Artificial Intelligence Help Improve Air Force Talent Management?

An Exploratory Application

DAVID SCHULKER, NELSON LIM, LUKE J. MATTHEWS, GEOFFREY E. GRIMM, ANTHONY LAWRENCE, PERRY SHAMEEM FIROZ

For more information on this publication, visit www.rand.org/t/RRA812-1

Library of Congress Cataloging-in-Publication Data is available for this publication.
ISBN: 978-1-9774-0645-3

Published by the RAND Corporation, Santa Monica, Calif.
© Copyright 2021 RAND Corporation
RAND® is a registered trademark.

Cover: U.S. Air Force/Tech. Sgt. Ken Bergmann; Adobe Stock/Siarhei.

Cover design: Peter Soriano

Support RAND
Make a tax-deductible charitable contribution at
www.rand.org/giving/contribute

www.rand.org

Preface

Both private and public organizations are increasingly taking advantage of improvements in computing power, data availability, and rapidly evolving analytic capabilities to improve business processes. Many of these improvements have affected how organizations shape their human capital through human resource management (HRM) policies. If implemented well, data-enabled policies can improve an organization's ability to recruit and retain the skill sets that they need, utilizing personnel in a way that takes maximal advantage of their capabilities. These trends have prompted U.S. Department of Defense policymakers to become more interested in whether adopting such methods would enable more-effective management of department personnel.

In this report, we explore one such application that would enable the U.S. Air Force to take a step forward in leveraging existing data for improved HRM policies and practices. Specifically, we develop a performance-scoring system that uses machine learning, which would enable the expanded use of performance narratives in HRM processes.

This report should be of interest to Department of Defense policymakers looking to modernize HRM policies by leveraging analytics or to those involved in areas related to the design and implementation of performance management systems. Although we focus on the Air Force, the concepts in this report could provide insight for those in the other armed services who face similar challenges in using officer performance information in force management decisions.

This research was conducted within the Manpower, Personnel, and Training Program of RAND Project AIR FORCE as part of the fiscal year 2019/2020 project Applying Machine Learning and Artificial Intelligence to Officer Evaluations.

RAND Project AIR FORCE

RAND Project AIR FORCE (PAF), a division of the RAND Corporation, is the Department of the Air Force's (DAF's) federally funded research and development center for studies and analyses, supporting both the United States Air Force and the United States Space Force. PAF provides the DAF with independent analyses of policy alternatives affecting the development, employment, combat readiness, and support of current and future air, space, and cyber forces. Research is conducted in four programs: Strategy and Doctrine; Force Modernization and Employment; Manpower, Personnel, and Training; and Resource Management.

Additional information about PAF is available on our website: www.rand.org/paf/

Funding

Funding for this research was made possible by the independent research and development provisions of RAND's contracts for the operation of its U.S. Department of Defense federally funded research and development centers.

Contents

Preface iii
Figures and Tables ix
Summary xi
Acknowledgments xv
Abbreviations xvii

CHAPTER ONE
Introduction 1
Artificial Intelligence and Human Resource Management 2
Conceptual Framework and Outline of the Report 3

CHAPTER TWO
The Business Need for Performance Metrics in Human Resource
    Management Decisions 7
Business Understanding Roadmap 7
Importance of Officer Evaluations in Human Resource Management
    Processes 7
Difficulty of Extracting Performance Information from Officer
    Records 8
How Artificial Intelligence Might Help Decisionmakers Get More
    from Officer Performance Records 9
How an Artificial Intelligence System Would Evaluate Performance
    Narratives 11
Artificial Intelligence Business Objective 13

CHAPTER THREE
Understanding Officer Evaluation System Data............................ 15
Data Understanding Roadmap.. 15
Data Requirements for the Proposed System 15
Structure of the Air Force's Officer Performance Report 16
Challenges for Data Extraction 17
Extracting Performance Narratives from Archived Forms................. 19
Linking Performance Narratives to Expert Assessments.................. 22
Assessment of Existing Data 24

CHAPTER FOUR
Processing Performance Narratives to Create Analytic Data 25
Data Preparation Roadmap... 25
Common Steps for Processing Textual Data for Machine Learning 25
Example of Processing Applied to Officer Performance Narratives 28
Potential Refinements for Improving Future Models....................... 30

CHAPTER FIVE
**Modeling the Relationship Between Performance Narratives and
    Promotion**... 31
Modeling Roadmap.. 31
Modeling Approaches for Linking Processed Performance Narratives
    to Promotion Outcomes.. 31
Model Validation.. 32
Modeling Results.. 33

CHAPTER SIX
Evaluating Other Implementation Considerations....................... 43
Evaluation Roadmap.. 43
Privacy... 43
Fairness.. 44
Explainability.. 46
Unintended Consequences of Implementation............................. 47

CHAPTER SEVEN

Conclusion and Policy Implications 49
Artificial Intelligence Performance-Scoring System Exploratory
    Assessment 49
Policy Implications 51
Conclusion 54

References 55

Figures and Tables

Figures

S.1. Exploratory Assessment of the Artificial Intelligence
Performance-Scoring System xiii
1.1. Cross-Industry Standard Process for Data-Mining.............. 3
3.1. Sample Officer Performance Report (Air Force Form 707) 17
3.2. Officer Performance Report Data Extract...................... 20
3.3. Schematic for a Relational Database Architecture to
Encode Officer Performance Report Data...................... 21
4.1. Example Data Preparation Steps for Officer Performance
Narratives... 29
5.1. Top Terms That Most Highly Correlate with the
Performance Index from O-5 Outcomes........................ 38
5.2. Top Terms That Most Highly Correlate with the
Performance Index from O-6 Outcomes 39
5.3. Change in Performance Index Associated with Adjusted
Performance Narrative Inputs.................................. 42
7.1. Exploratory Assessment of the Artificial Intelligence
Performance-Scoring System 50

Tables

5.1. Model Results 33
5.2. Percentage of O-5 Candidates Who Remain in the Same
Percentile Group over Time 36
5.3. Percentage of O-6 Candidates Who Remain in the Same
Percentile Group over Time 36

Summary

Issue

Each year, the U.S. Air Force uses standardized Officer Performance Reports to record descriptions of each officer's job responsibilities and accomplishments. Air Force human resource management (HRM) practices could incorporate this rich information into more processes, except that gleaning the information requires a panel of experienced officers to read and interpret the content. An artificial intelligence (AI)-enabled performance-scoring system that mimics the process by which human experts judge performance narratives could help senior leaders take full advantage of performance records when making talent management decisions.

Approach

In an attempt to develop such a tool, we applied the cross-industry standard process for data-mining (CRISP-DM), an established framework for solving data-mining problems, to the concept of an AI performance-scoring system. If such a system can faithfully replicate the judgments of experienced officers, it would have the potential to quickly translate a narrative into a quantitative performance index. This analysis could turn out to be a useful first step toward meeting a business need, but it also serves as a *worked example* (i.e., a step-by-step solution to a problem) to guide Air Force policymakers as they consider how to approach the many potential ways in which AI can improve HRM processes.

Findings

- Figure S.1 summarizes the steps in the CRISP-DM and the inputs and outputs of each step of the process in our analysis. It also highlights the steps where our experience indicates that Air Force practitioners could encounter challenges with this or similar applications.
- There is a business need for the AI performance-scoring system. The system could be used as a tool to facilitate policy analysis, assist development teams, enable professional development, or aid in competitive selection decisions.
- Extracting and digitizing large amounts of officer evaluation data from the existing archive is feasible, but, because the process of digitizing the text from older documents requires extensive tuning and computation time, the process could present a potential challenge to future efforts by Air Force practitioners.
- Initial model results are promising: Standard machine-learning algorithms accurately predicted record quality by identifying known performance signals in the text without explicit programming.
- The evaluation phase revealed that implementation concerns regarding privacy, fairness, explainability, and other unintended consequences are greatest if the system were used to make decisions that would alter officers' careers. These considerations could be less of a barrier to implementing the system for other purposes.

Implications

- Policymakers should position systems and policies to take advantage of analytic uses of data that HRM processes generate.
- Natural language processing techniques can reduce the need to pre-quantify information at the data collection stage.
- Human resources managers should consider AI applications to be an enabler of better policies rather than a substitute for human decisionmaking.

Figure S.1
Exploratory Assessment of the Artificial Intelligence Performance-Scoring System

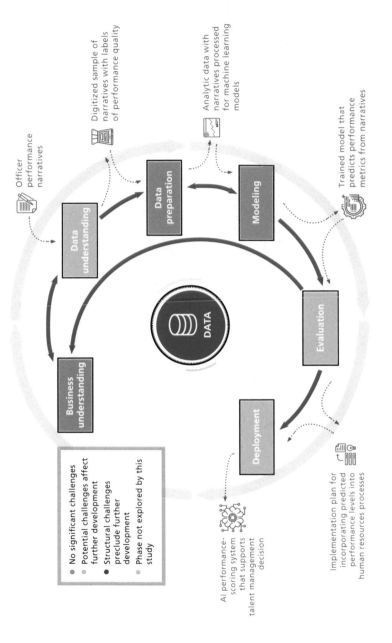

Officer performance narratives

Digitized sample of narratives with labels of performance quality

Analytic data with narratives processed for machine learning models

Trained model that predicts performance metrics from narratives

Implementation plan for incorporating predicted performance levels into human resources processes

AI performance-scoring system that supports talent management decision

Data understanding

Data preparation

Modeling

Evaluation

Deployment

Business understanding

DATA

- No significant challenges
- Potential challenges affect further development
- Structural challenges preclude further development
- Phase not explored by this study

Acknowledgments

We are extremely grateful for the support of members of the Air Force personnel community, without whom we would not have been able to access the data to perform this exploratory analysis. We thank Lt Gen Brian Kelly, Maj Gen Robert LaBrutta, Gregory Parsons, and Jerry Diaz in the Manpower, Personnel, and Services office for supporting our data request. We are also grateful to Lt Col Thomas Newlon, David Philpott, and Roger Foley at the Air Force Personnel Center for their cooperation and assistance in understanding current Air Force efforts. We appreciate the help of Maj Cory Steinbrecher, 2d Lt Ricky Wilder, and the automated records management system developers who provided information on current and future data systems and executed our data pull, as well as Paul Emslie and Judy Mele at RAND for helping coordinate the data transfer. And we are extremely grateful to John Sabo and Steve Harris at the Air Force Personnel Center for their continued assistance with the project.

We also appreciate the thoughtful comments and assistance of our peer reviewers, Matt Walsh and Lisa Harrington. We are grateful for the support of RAND's Internal Research and Development program managers, including Susan Marquis, Howard Shatz, and Lisa Jaycox. And we appreciate the patience and persistent support of RAND Project AIR FORCE leaders, including Ted Harshberger and Ray Conley, without whom the effort could not have succeeded.

Abbreviations

AI	artificial intelligence
ANN	artificial neural network
ARMS	automated records management system
CRISP-DM	cross-industry standard process for data-mining
DoD	U.S. Department of Defense
HR	human resources
HRM	human resource management
HTML	Hypertext Markup Language
ML	machine learning
NLP	natural language processing
OES	Officer Evaluation System
O-5	lieutenant colonel
O-6	colonel
OPR	Officer Performance Report
PDF	Portable Document Format
SVM	support vector machine
TFIDF	term frequency–inverse document frequency

CHAPTER ONE

Introduction

The abilities of computers to perform tasks that previously required human intelligence are rapidly increasing, so much so that there are regular news reports of technology firms successfully performing complex cognitive tasks with a computer program. In this report, we refer to these capabilities as *artificial intelligence* (AI). Dramatic progress over the past two decades in the field of machine learning (ML) has fueled many AI breakthroughs and accelerated the pace at which AI can automate or streamline work processes (Jordan and Mitchell, 2015).[1]

Advances in ML have fundamentally altered the development of AI systems. Before the recent progress in ML, creating a computer program capable of performing an intelligent task required the programmer to enumerate each rule governing the computer's decisions. This manual process significantly limited the complexity of tasks within reach of AI. Now, ML algorithms merely need rich data—that is, cases to train the system, coupled with desired outputs from the programmer—and the program discovers the rules using feedback from the desired decisions (Brynjolfsson and Mitchell, 2017). Improvements in raw computing power, the volume and quality of data, and the algorithms themselves have brought computer functionality to a level at which it can approximate tasks involving image recognition or even make interactive phone calls in natural language.

---

[1] *AI* broadly refers to any application that uses software to mimic a human performing a task. *ML* refers to technical approaches to AI that use statistical algorithms that use examples to learn how the system should behave, as opposed to an AI system that is programmed to follow a set of explicit rules.

Artificial Intelligence and Human Resource Management

The promise of AI technologies has motivated many organizations, including the U.S. Department of Defense (DoD), to push toward wider adoption (DoD, 2018a). Yet, relatively few firms have succeeded in shifting toward the practices that support broad AI adoption (Fountaine, McCarthy, and Saleh, 2019). Furthermore, among the broader set of processes in which AI could help firms become more efficient or productive, human resource management (HRM) processes present unique challenges to AI adoption. HRM decisions are highly consequential for individual lives, so AI adopters must carefully address numerous ethical challenges. Given these barriers, only a minority of firms report that they have adopted analytics in HRM at all (Tambe, Cappelli, and Yakubovich, 2019).

DoD's AI strategy exhorts its organizations to "identify, prioritize, and select new AI mission initiatives systematically, and then execute an initial sequence of cross-functional use cases that demonstrate value and spur momentum" (DoD, 2018a, p. 9). Although AI does have the potential to improve HRM business processes, it can be difficult for policymakers to discern which proposed projects have high prospects for success in HRM and which are inherently problematic. To assist Air Force policymakers, we explore one possible application of AI to HRM by using a systematic process to investigate whether AI could fill a key information gap in the performance management system. Specifically, we explore the feasibility and usefulness of developing a system that can automatically process the performance information in an officer's records and produce a performance metric. The ability to derive a performance metric from an officer's records has many potential uses, which we describe in this report. The main purpose of this exploration, however, is to serve as a *worked example* (i.e., a step-by-step solution to a problem) for Air Force policymakers as they consider how to approach the potential ways in which AI can improve HRM processes.

Conceptual Framework and Outline of the Report

We ground our investigation of an AI-enabled performance-scoring system in the most widely used process model for solving data-mining problems: the cross-industry standard process for data-mining (CRISP-DM) (Chapman et al., 2000).[2] The CRISP-DM structures the problem-solving process as a life cycle that includes six phases (Figure 1.1).

Figure 1.1
Cross-Industry Standard Process for Data-Mining

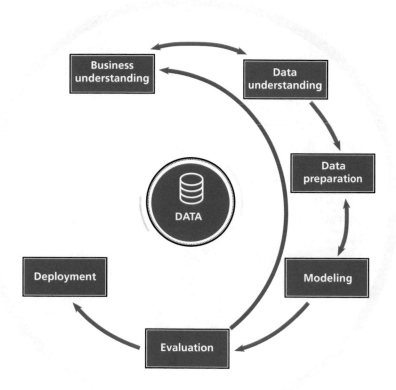

SOURCE: Adapted from Chapman et al., 2000, p. 10.

---

[2]   See Mariscal, Marban, and Fernandez, 2010, for a review of data-mining and knowledge-discovery process models and methodologies.

In the *business understanding* phase (which is the focus of Chapter Two), analysts define the project objectives, goals, and success criteria from a business perspective and assess the requirements, risks, costs, and benefits of the proposed project.

In the *data understanding* phase (Chapter Three), analysts examine the structure of the data and the process that generated the data and then acquire and explore the data and identify potential quality problems (which might result in returning to the prior phase to revise the project objectives and problem formulation). The main goals of this phase for the current application are to determine whether it is feasible to extract the officer performance information from existing databases, whether enough data are available to permit an AI analysis, and whether the performance information can be matched to valid outcome metrics for quality. If feasible, the data understanding phase should result in a digitized file containing the narratives describing each officer's performance, as well as labels (e.g., scores or order-of-merit rankings) denoting associated levels of performance. At the end of the data understanding phase, the performance information would still be in the form of narrative descriptions.

The *data preparation* phase (Chapter Four) includes activities that process the textual data from the data understanding phase, converting the narratives into quantitative data suitable for modeling with ML algorithms.

In the *modeling* phase (Chapter Five), analysts apply different ML algorithms and measure their predictive effectiveness in order to develop the data-mining system that can ingest performance narratives and produce an informative score representing an officer's performance level. Attempts to model the data often reveal that additional data preparation is needed, and this back-and-forth workflow is represented by the two-way arrow between the modeling and data preparation phases in Figure 1.1.

After analysts arrive at a model that functions well from an analytic perspective, in the *evaluation* phase, they must thoroughly evaluate the operations of the model and consider other factors that might affect implementation and, subsequently, *deployment* (the last phase of the CRISP-DM). We discuss these considerations in Chapter Six and then summarize and conclude the exploratory assessment in Chapter Seven.

To ensure that this report fulfills its purpose as a worked example, we include enough detail in each chapter for Air Force practitioners to follow a similar process on this or other cases of AI adoption. We begin each chapter with a roadmap section that highlights the major steps and conclusions in each stage of the CRISP-DM so that the policy audience can follow the example without delving into the nuanced methodological hurdles that we encountered in this application.

CHAPTER TWO

The Business Need for Performance Metrics in Human Resource Management Decisions

Business Understanding Roadmap

- Air Force policy acknowledges that officer evaluations are an important input into many HRM processes, but the fact that evaluations take the form of bulleted narratives makes them difficult to process and apply to policy decisions.
- An AI system that can quantify the performance information in performance narratives can help improve the effectiveness of HRM policy.
- The quantified outputs of an AI performance-scoring system can be useful for evaluating other HRM policies, guiding the efforts of development teams, or assisting with competitive selection decisions. The AI system can also be used as a teaching tool.
- The Air Force can meet this business need by using computerized processing of natural language to link performance narratives to a set of labels that specify which narratives describe higher or lower performance levels.

Importance of Officer Evaluations in Human Resource Management Processes

Organizations implement performance management systems to steer employee work activities toward the organization's mission and to improve organizational performance (Aguinis, 2013, p. 3). Air Force policy sets the rules for performance management through the Officer Evaluation System (OES), in which supervisors (known as *raters*) establish standards and expectations for subordinates (known as *ratees*) and curate feedback and development to better conform each service member's performance to organizational goals (Department of the Air Force, 2020a). Typically, each officer receives initial and midpoint feedback from his or her rater before receiving an annual Officer Performance Report (OPR) that documents the officer's accomplishments at the end of the cycle.[1]

In addition to their direct use in the performance review cycle, records of individual performance provide important input into a variety of HRM decisions. Air Force policy states that officer ratings "provide information for making promotion recommendation, selection, or propriety action; selective continuation; involuntary separation; selective early retirement; assignment; school nomination and selection; and other management decisions" (Department of the Air Force, 2020a, p. 71). To wisely manage the talent inventory, then, decisionmakers depend on the information produced by the performance management system.

Difficulty of Extracting Performance Information from Officer Records

The main vehicle for documenting how an Air Force officer performs in each year of his or her career is the OPR, where raters comment on ratee performance in bulleted essay form.[2] The narrative comments on performance offer raters flexibility in communicating nuanced feedback,

---

[1]   The Air Force does not currently archive the initial and midpoint feedback forms. Certain circumstances, such as when an officer's rater changes during the cycle, require the completion of an OPR outside of the normal annual timetable.

[2]   At the time of this report, the Air Force was investigating a new OPR format that combines a narrative essay portion with a section containing behaviorally anchored rating scales (similar to the format used in the Navy and Marine Corps). Our understanding is that all formats under consideration will continue to have an essay section in which raters can communicate performance information to human resources (HR) decisionmakers, which means that the topics discussed in this report will continue to apply.

which is helpful given the sensitive nature of the information (Brutus, 2010). However, narrative comments are more difficult to summarize and interpret than quantitative performance rating scales are. Most military performance narratives generally sound very positive in tone, but formal and informal processes have evolved whereby certain words and recommendations signal gradations of performance to HR decisionmakers (Wolfgeher, 2009). In the Marine Corps, for instance, such words and phrases as "capable," "retain," and "promote with peers" are known as *velvet daggers* because they sound positive to ratees while indicating sub-par performance to promotion boards (Tierney, 2019). Possibly because raters are trying to make the feedback more palatable to ratees (Brutus, 2010), the narratives for lower-performing officers rarely contain direct statements describing poor performance and instead simply omit the specific indicators of superior performance. Thus, a more generic narrative actually signals poor performance.

Such practices might be effective in communicating performance information to decisionmakers, but an unintended consequence is that the only way to discern the performance signals is for an experienced officer to read and judge the records. This requirement for human cognition places limits on the ability of HRM processes to incorporate systematic performance information. Only highly experienced officers are qualified to judge the records of others, and even their judgments might be inconsistent depending on differences in individual experiences. For this reason, multiple officers typically review the same set of records when a candidate is being selected for a promotion or key position. In sum, when HR managers want to rank officer performance among a large group to aid in selection decisions, ensuring fairness and consistency in those rankings requires many staff-hours of expert time.

How Artificial Intelligence Might Help Decisionmakers Get More from Officer Performance Records

A well-calibrated AI system could help senior leaders take full advantage of officer performance records in their talent management decisions by supplementing or streamlining the manual process of sifting through performance records. To differentiate the topic of this report from many other possible ways to apply AI to OES data, we consider the following narrowly tailored concept: an AI system that can read the performance narratives written for a group of officers and return an index measuring each service member's level of performance. This system would simulate the judgment of an experienced officer if he or she were asked to go through a set of records to determine which ones indicate the highest levels of performance. This functionality fits squarely within the goals articulated in DoD's AI strategy, which seeks to harness "the ability of AI to reduce inefficiencies from manual, laborious, data-centric tasks . . . with the objective of simplifying workflows and improving the speed and accuracy of repetitive tasks" (DoD, 2018a, p. 6). An AI performance index has at least four applications.

A performance index could serve as an outcome for evaluating other HRM policies. The main goal of HRM is to improve organizational performance. Thus, nearly every operation in the HRM life cycle (e.g., recruitment, hiring, training, retention) would benefit from having individual performance metrics by which to assess progress. Yet the narrative form of performance evaluations makes them difficult to process, so decisionmakers rarely use such information to judge the effectiveness of recruitment, retention, or other policies. An AI-generated performance index could fill this gap and spur improvements to HRM policies.

A performance index could help inform development policy. The Air Force currently uses the development team construct—as outlined in Air Force Instruction 36-2670 (see Department of the Air Force, 2020b)—to oversee officer education, training, and experiences in view of current and future mission requirements. Development teams could benefit from an improved understanding of officer performance so that they can better tailor their development of those service members. Furthermore, an important responsibility of development teams is to "review the demographic makeup of the functional community and identify potential barriers to all Airmen reaching their highest potential" (Department of the Air Force, 2020b, p. 22). The ability to monitor and address any negative performance trends for demographic subgroups would also help development teams be more effective at their mission.

The AI system could be used as a training tool. An AI system's ability to draw on a large body of historical performance narratives to evaluate new writing could, in itself, be a useful training and development tool for raters who will judge ratees' performance. Sustaining the OES as a system that accurately communicates performance information requires experienced officers to teach junior officers the nuances of Air Force writing. An AI system that can evaluate performance narratives in real time could help provide feedback during training or professional military education.

A performance index could be used for competitive selection decisions. Deciding whether to use an algorithm in high-stakes decisions that could significantly affect individual careers will require serious consideration of whether those affected perceive the system to be fair and transparent (Tambe, Cappelli, and Yakubovich, 2019), and we will discuss these issues in more detail later in this report. But a list of possible uses of such a system would not be complete without including the system's potential to inform selection decisions at any level, provided that concerns related to bias and accuracy could be adequately addressed.

How an Artificial Intelligence System Would Evaluate Performance Narratives

Success in this task requires engineering an AI system that replicates the qualitative judgments of humans when they read a specific text. For example, a human can easily read a job advertisement from a restaurant and decide whether the position advertised is for a chef or a server. A human would classify the advertisement by reading it and interpreting the language in light of what he or she already knows about restaurants. In this simple example, one could develop an AI system that approximates the human's judgment by giving an ML algorithm many example advertisements and letting it find key terms and language structures that are highly correlated with one job or the other.

An automated essay scoring system in the education domain is an example that more closely resembles the AI performance-scoring system for Air Force performance narratives that we focus on in this report (Murphy, 2019; Zhang, 2013). Reading and scoring written essays requires time, and only certain education personnel have the training and experience to accurately perform the task. Automated essay scoring systems help expand the availability of performance feedback for writing in cases when the labor required for humans to evaluate a large volume of essays renders their use infeasible.

The current application of predicting expert evaluations of officer performance narratives falls under the subdomain known as *supervised ML*, because it derives scoring rules from thousands of examples of textual documents that have been pre-labeled by human judgment. The pre-labeled examples (i.e., the training data) "supervise" the algorithm by providing feedback on the quality of its predictions as it learns patterns that predict the labeled examples. The research literature commonly denotes such applications of supervised ML to text data as a form of *natural language processing* (NLP).

This explanation of NLP clarifies the fact that NLP does not involve a computer naturally processing language the same way that a human would; rather, it entails a computerized processing of natural language. The ML process that the computer follows bears only limited resemblance to the mechanisms by which humans learn language. In a typical NLP application, the computer comes to each problem completely naïve. It has no innate sense of grammar, and it has no sense of the meaning of words—that is, no sense of what external things they signify. Thus, teaching a computer to predict an outcome from a body of text begins by breaking the text down into components and features that statistically correlate with the phenomena it is trying to predict. Then, the computer uses the information signifying gradations of performance to create rules that allow it to mimic a human performing the same task.

Artificial Intelligence Business Objective

This brief review of the OES suggests a business need for analytic tools that can help with the labor-intensive process of reading and judging officer performance narratives. The business objective of this application, then, is to develop an AI system capable of taking performance narratives as an input and producing a performance metric as an output. At this stage, the concept appears suitable for ML techniques that take free-form text as inputs and attempt to predict a quantitative output. In the next chapter, we explore the availability of suitable data to meet this business need.

CHAPTER THREE

Understanding Officer Evaluation System Data

Data Understanding Roadmap

- Developing an AI system that can quantify the information in officer performance narratives requires a large sample of narratives and a data source for labels that denote the level of performance that the narratives describe.
- We assembled a large sample of performance narratives from Air Force records, but the current data storage procedures required extensive processing to digitize the text on each OPR form. This processing step could present a challenge to practitioners using OES data for other applications.
- There are several existing data sources for performance labels, including records from promotion boards, developmental education boards, and command selection boards. We chose to explore the usefulness of promotion board decisions to inform the AI scoring system.
- Using promotion results for this system has some notable limitations, so we recommend that practitioners consider several additional methods to help refine the labels over time.

Data Requirements for the Proposed System

As shown in the CRISP-DM in Figure 1.1, valid, reliable, and accessible data are at the center of the development of an AI performance-scoring system. The developer of the system needs to train it to recognize terms and language structures that indicate gradations of performance from the text of Air Force performance narratives. This task requires two primary data inputs: (1) a sufficiently large sample of officer performance narratives and (2) outcome labels that provide information about which narratives indicate the best job performance. The labels can come from either preexisting assessments of the performance narratives (such as records from promotion boards) or expert judgments that were generated for the purpose of training the ML algorithm. By associating the narratives with the previous or preferred outcome, the machine can be trained to mimic the expert judgments by distinguishing the bits of text that indicate good performance from those associated with lesser performance or those that do not convey performance-related information at all. In this chapter, we assess the availability, quality, and accessibility of data that would be suitable for this task.

Structure of the Air Force's Officer Performance Report

The structure of the OPR has changed over time, but the modes that raters use to convey information have been consistent. A typical OPR has the following sections: ratee identification data, job description, performance factors, rater overall assessment, additional rater overall assessment, and reviewer, among others. The rater overall assessment and the additional rater overall assessment sections contain the primary performance narratives. Inputs from raters in these sections are mandatory, and the overall assessment "allows evaluators to comment on the ratee's overall performance and performance-based potential as compared to others in the same grade known by the evaluators" (Department of the Air Force, 2020a, p. 91). Figure 3.1 shows the first page on an OPR and sample comments in the sections previously mentioned. For the July 2015 version of the OPR (the most recent at time of writing), a minimum of one line is required for each assessment section, but the rater overall assessment section can have a maximum number of only six lines, and the additional rater overall assessment section can have a maximum of only four lines.

Figure 3.1
Sample Officer Performance Report (Air Force Form 707)

OFFICER PERFORMANCE REPORT *(Lt thru Col)*					
I. RATEE IDENTIFICATION DATA *(Read AFI 36-2406 carefully before filling in any item)*					
1. NAME *(Last, First, Middle Initial)* Doe, John S	2. SSN 123-45-6789	3. RANK Capt	4. DAFSC 21A4	5. REASON FOR REPORT Annual	6. PAS CODE QWERTY
7. ORGANIZATION, COMMAND, LOCATION, AND COMPONENT HQ Air Force Personnel Center (AFPC) Randolph AFB TX (AD)				8. PERIOD OF REPORT FROM 2 Jan 2018 THRU 1 Jan 2019	9. NO. DAYS SUPV. 300 NO. DAYS NON-RATED 46
II. JOB DESCRIPTION *(Limit text to 4 lines)* DUTY TITLE Programs OIC					10. SRID 1R847
- Spearheaded quality of life improvements--pay table reform, retirement redux repeal, significant pay raise - Garnered over $200M for new family housing, $225M for housing allowances, and increased bonuses - Led $22M program through Congressional minefield--tenaciously protected MILSTAR follow-on program - Restored $15M to CSAF/SECAF priority--without his expert guidance, the program would have folded					

III. PERFORMANCE FACTORS	DOES NOT MEET STANDARDS	MEETS STANDARDS
Job Knowledge, Leadership Skills (to include Promoting a Healthy Organizational Climate), Professional Qualities, Organizational Skills, Judgment and Decisions, Communication Skills (see reverse if marked Does Not Meet Standards)	☐	☒

IV. RATER OVERALL ASSESSMENT *(Limit text to 6 lines)*
- Led efforts that resulted in historic gains for our Airmen and kept AF readiness at the forefront in Congress
- Developed MAJCOM Top Readiness Concerns brief for OSD--provided the real story on AF readiness
- Guided analysis of impact of long-term contingency operations on Air Force people, budget, and equipment
- Protected programs vital to AF future--AF lead for C-5 engine upgrade, $200M effort--flawless execution
- Authored $10M budget proposal and defended to Congress on the Hill--program fully funded as a result
- Forged DoD-wide definition of TEMPO for $100M Congressional Report on Personnel TEMPO legislation

Last performance feedback was accomplished on: 13 Jun 2018   (IAW AFI 36-2406) (If not accomplished, state the reason)

NAME, GRADE, BR OF SVC, ORGN, COMMAND & LOCATION Fname1 Lname1, Maj, USAF HQ Air Force Personnel Center (AFPC) Randolph AFB, TX	DUTY TITLE Chief, Programs Branch	DATE
	SSN 1111	SIGNATURE

V. ADDITIONAL RATER OVERALL ASSESSMENT *(Limit text to 4 lines)*   ☒ CONCUR   ☐ NON-CONCUR
- Designed future AF concept team for implementation--avoided over $18K in contracted cost to Air Force
- Selected to brief Congressional panel--never missed a beat--personally saved $15M multi-year contract
- Number 2 of my 45 action officers--trusted and respected--send to operational command after IDE in-res
- Truly superb staff officer and leader--directorate's go-to guy for toughest financial management issues

NAME, GRADE, BR OF SVC, ORGN, COMMAND & LOCATION Fname2 Lname2, Lt Col, USAF HQ Air Force Personnel Center (AFPC) Randolph AFB, TX	DUTY TITLE Chief, Programs Division	DATE
	SSN 2222	SIGNATURE

VI. REVIEWER *(If required, limit text to 3 lines)*	☒ CONCUR	☐ NON-CONCUR

SOURCE: Author sample text on Air Force Form 707, available at Air Reserve Personnel Center, undated.

Challenges for Data Extraction

Under current OES processes, raters compose performance narratives in an electronic form that is moved from person to person to collect inputs and digital signatures from all involved parties as part of the evaluation cycle. Although OPRs are initially composed in digital forms, the records are ultimately archived in a database as Portable Document Format (PDF) files or images of documents. Until around 2007, all OPRs were stored as images—even when the information was entered into an editable PDF file or other computerized form—because the approval processes for these forms had not been made electronic. Thus, electronic forms were commonly printed and then passed around for multiple signatures, whereupon the signed printed forms would be entered into the OPR database. Today, all OPR data-entry and approval processes are digital, but finalized OPRs are still converted into a noneditable PDF file before being entered into the OPR database.

Regardless of the format of the archived OPRs (i.e., PDF or image file), the forms are indexed by metadata (i.e., data external to the forms, which capture information about the forms that can be used to access them in the database). The metadata include the service member's name, Social Security Number, a document identification number, and the document date. These metadata, until recently, were manually entered, but new processes collect them electronically with character recognition software. The textual data in the OPRs are all retained by this process, but the text is not searchable or indexable. Because the OPR database system can be queried using only the metadata that are explicitly attached to each file (and not the data contained inside each file), analysts cannot search, for example, for all the forms using a particular word or acronym. In addition, formatting has changed multiple times over the years, which complicates the process of extracting information from the OPRs.

In our discussions with stakeholders and database managers at the Air Force Personnel Center, we found that it would be possible to pull historical OPR records from the Automated Records Management System for a large body of officers, and those data could serve as inputs into an AI system. The documents are already regularly accessed by other systems, such as the electronic Board Operations Support System used for promotion boards. Analysts at the Air Force Personnel Center also indicated an interest in applying analytics to the text of historical OPRs as part of their analyses of promotion boards, but at the time of this study, they were still working with data owners to develop a customized way to query the database that met their needs.

Extracting Performance Narratives from Archived Forms

For this exploratory analysis, we requested all performance records for 18,851 officers who had met with O-5 (lieutenant colonel) or O-6 (colonel) promotion boards in the ten-year period from 2009 to 2018, which included 241,936 documents. After receiving the raw records, the next step was to extract the performance narratives (and other useful information, such as the performance period) from the forms and store the information for the analysis. Although the officers had met with a promotion board fairly recently, the performance records dated as far back as the early 1990s. Accurately extracting the performance narratives across the various types of forms and digital formats was a significant challenge.

We opted to use Python, an open-sourced programming language, for this task because it offered a wide variety of text-processing software packages. Also, the Conda environment manager enabled us to design and test the software before implementing programs on the raw data in a secure computing environment. For the OPRs in PDF format, we converted the PDF files into Hypertext Markup Language (HTML) files and extracted the data from the HTML files using built-in HTML tags and regular expressions. For the OPRs that were stored as images, we converted the image files to text files using optical character recognition and extracted the required data using regular expressions. Because the images varied greatly in resolution and quality, this was an iterative process and required a period of tuning before we could be confident that the programs were accurately processing the text. Even after we successfully tested programs that could process the text, executing the task required extensive computational resources (especially for the image files, which required significantly more processing time). Although it is difficult to parse out the processing time from the tuning and troubleshooting, we estimate that extracting all text took 20 days, in total, running in parallel on up to four machines.

Figure 3.2 shows an example of how this process would have taken the sample OPR from Figure 3.1 and converted it into a digitized table amenable to the next step in the process.

Figure 3.2
Officer Performance Report Data Extract

ssn	start_dt	end_dt	index	text
123456789	01,02,2018	01,01,2019	job_description_0	Spearheaded quality of life improvements--pay table reform, retirement redux repeal, significant pay raise
123456789	01,02,2018	01,01,2019	job_description_1	Garnered over $200M for new family housing, $225M for housing allowances, and increased bonuses
123456789	01,02,2018	01,01,2019	job_description_2	Led $22M program through Congressional minefield--tenaciously protected MILSTAR follow-on program
123456789	01,02,2018	01,01,2019	job_description_3	Restored $15M to CSAF/SECAF priority--without his expert guidance, the program would have folded
123456789	01,02,2018	01,01,2019	primary_rater_0	Led efforts that resulted in historic gains for our Airmen and kept AF readiness at the forefront in Congress
123456789	01,02,2018	01,01,2019	primary_rater_1	Developed MAJCOM Top Readiness Concerns brief for OSD--provided the real story on AF readiness
123456789	01,02,2018	01,01,2019	primary_rater_2	Guided analysis of impact of long-term contingency operations on Air Force people, budget, and equipment
123456789	01,02,2018	01,01,2019	primary_rater_3	Protected programs vital to AF future--AF lead for C-5 engine upgrade, $200M effort--flawless execution
123456789	01,02,2018	01,01,2019	primary_rater_4	Authored $10M budget proposal and defended to Congress on the Hill--program fully funded as a result
123456789	01,02,2018	01,01,2019	primary_rater_5	Forged DoD-wide definition of TEMPO for $100M Congressional Report on Personnel TEMPO legislation
123456789	01,02,2018	01,01,2019	additional_rater_0	Designed future AF concept team for implementation--avoided over $18K in contracted cost to Air Force
123456789	01,02,2018	01,01,2019	additional_rater_1	Selected to brief Congressional panel--never missed a beat--personally saved $15M multi-year contract
123456789	01,02,2018	01,01,2019	additional_rater_2	Number 2 of my 45 action officers--trusted and respected--send to operational command after IDE in-res
123456789	01,02,2018	01,01,2019	additional_rater_3	Truly superb staff officer and leader--directorateâ€™s go-to guy for toughest financial management issues

The step of extracting the data from performance forms could be automated or eliminated by information technology changes that store new performance data in a way that is available for analytic purposes. Ongoing modernization efforts intended to streamline the performance evaluation process could store all of the information in a relational database so that analysts can efficiently retrieve it. Such databases can be encoded in multiple database languages, such as SQL and Oracle, but all should consist of a set of tables that are interconnected through identifiers. Figure 3.3 depicts a simple relational database: The top table includes the individual lines of text. Those lines of text then link to individual OPRs that are indexed in a separate table, which links to individuals in the third table on the bottom right. Storing the information in this way would enable various HR analysts to retrieve it efficiently and securely at the level needed for each task. For instance, analyses focused on summarizing the job activities of a population of officers would need to draw on only the first table, without linking personal data to individuals or career outcomes.

Figure 3.3
Schematic for a Relational Database Architecture to Encode Officer Performance Report Data

Primary Key	Bullet Text	Bullet Number	Reviewer
randomNumber1	Excellent work product ...	1	1
randomNumber2	Keen insights ...	2	1
randomNumber3	Didn't know ...	3	1
randomNumber4	Could work on ...	4	2

Primary Key	OPR#
randomNumber1	OPR1
randomNumber2	OPR1
randomNumber3	OPR1
randomNumber4	OPR2

OPR#	Person#
OPR1	ID1
OPR2	ID1

Linking Performance Narratives to Expert Assessments

Air Force OPRs contain descriptions of officers' performance, but training a performance-scoring algorithm also requires information on which narratives indicate higher levels of job performance. Put another way, the AI system needs supplementary data that *label* the quality of performance described in each narrative. Existing sources of such information include official boards that review and assess the overall performance of officers and select them for different opportunities based on merit. By combining the performance descriptions with these career outcomes, the developer of the performance-scoring system can train a machine to recognize the subtle signs of gradations in performance. The ML algorithm would use the feedback from the labels to learn rules for assigning higher performance scores to OPRs that are similar to OPRs of superior performers.

There are three boards of experts that evaluate a large number of officer records and whose results could thus be potential data sources and theoretically provide suitable labels for the current application. These three boards are promotion boards, developmental education boards, and command selection boards. Results from promotion boards were the most readily available to us, so we opted to use promotion outcomes to train the initial models in this AI system. However, a key part of the data understanding stage is to grasp the implications of this decision for the resulting system.

Potential Drawbacks of Using Promotion Results as Outcome Labels

When selecting which officers to elevate to a higher position, promotion boards score individual records and rank them according to general merit, which makes the boards' rankings an ideal source of information for an AI system to replicate. However, using promotion results has several drawbacks. First, the ideal outcome labels would be scores or complete order-of-merit rankings that would help differentiate narratives across the entire spectrum of performance quality. This metric is unavailable for promotion boards because current policies preclude the release of board scores or order-of-merit rankings for research and do not archive them for future analysis. The next-best option is to use the final selection outcome instead of the board scores, but this would discard useful information. Compared with board scores, selection outcomes (i.e., selected versus not selected) for groups of service members with high selection rates would not differentiate performance very well. For junior and middle grades, such as O-3 (captain) and O-4 (major), promotion rates can be close to 100 percent, which renders them useless for training an ML algorithm to differentiate quality. The promotion milestones where there is more differentiation happen much later in an officer's career, which means that an AI system that uses the information might not work well for more-junior officers.

A second drawback of using promotion results to inform the AI system about the quality of an officer's performance is that promotion boards spend a limited amount of time reviewing performance narratives. Because of time constraints, the boards tend to focus on a summary document known as a Promotion Recommendation Form, which contains some highlights from previous OPR narratives. But this process of summarizing the information in an officer's records for promotion boards could also limit the ability of the AI system to differentiate among performance narratives.

A final limitation of using promotion results to inform the AI system is that the model will tend to be backward-looking, which could limit its applicability to inform policy going forward. The degree to which this is a problem will depend on the stability of performance indicators over time relative to how quickly new data become available (Brynjolfsson and Mitchell, 2017). If the performance indicators change rapidly over time but these changes are slow to influence late-career promotion boards, then other information would be required to generate labels to inform the AI system.

Options to Address the Shortcomings of Using Promotion Results as Outcome Labels

There are other potential options to address these shortcomings. Further analyses could draw on information from other boards that might not have the same shortcomings. For instance, some developmental education boards make decisions earlier in an officer's career, so the results of those boards might adapt more rapidly to changes in performance narratives. In addition, scores or order-of-merit information from these boards might be easier to secure for research and analysis. A second option would be to generate new data specifically to improve the ML algorithm. The Air Force could survey experienced officers and ask them to evaluate sample performance narratives to generate new examples to inform the ML algorithm. One additional approach that would help address the potential for changes in the performance signals over time is to provide ongoing feedback to the ML algorithm so that it can improve over time. This approach is sometimes known as the *learning apprentice* or *human in the loop* because the AI system setup allows it to learn from observing human decisions while capturing ongoing decisions as additional examples (Brynjolfsson and Mitchell, 2017). Thus, even if the initial ML algorithm trained on promotion board decisions was highly imperfect, the algorithm could improve over time by incorporating new feedback from the system's users.

Assessment of Existing Data

The availability, quality, and accessibility of the performance data could limit or preclude the development of an AI performance-scoring system. The current practice of storing OPRs as images in the database system adds a layer of complexity to extracting performance descriptions from the OPRs. Although this practice is not optimal for analytics, it is still possible to extract a sufficiently large sample of records, convert the information in the forms into digitized data, and link the performance information to expert assessments of performance for the purpose of training an AI system to recognize patterns in the narratives that indicate different performance levels.

CHAPTER FOUR

Processing Performance Narratives to Create Analytic Data

Data Preparation Roadmap

- Creating a system that can quantify the performance level indicated in a body of text requires that the text be transformed into a quantitative form suitable for an ML model.
- The *bag-of-words approach* (so known because it strips the text of the syntactic relationship between words) breaks the text down into word fragments so that the ML algorithm can identify key words or phrases that predict promotion decisions.
- This approach forms a sensible starting point, but more-complex NLP techniques are also available. Future efforts can judge the value of these richer techniques by the degree to which they perform better than this baseline.

Common Steps for Processing Textual Data for Machine Learning

We applied NLP techniques to the OPR narratives by constructing a data matrix with a row for each individual's record and a column for each word that occurs in the entire body of documents. Typical applications of NLP proceed to *stem* the words, which means that endings such as *-ed* or *-s* are removed to arrive at just the root word. Thus, *walked, walks,* and *walk* would be all considered the same variable and coded in a single column in standard NLP approaches. It is also common to remove *stop words*. Stop words are lists compiled by linguists that are mere helper words in a given language and that indicate little about meaning. Examples of English stop words include *the, a, and,* and so forth, although they could be augmented with additional terms that are specific to the Air Force. We tested stemming and stop-word removal on our data but ultimately omitted these steps because they did not improve performance in the modeling stage.

In addition to including a column that represents each word that occurs in the data, it is also possible to include columns for group-ings of two words (*bigrams*), three words (*trigrams*), or any prespecified number words (*N-grams*) so that the modeling can explore key phrases in addition to terms. When applied to OPRs, for example, including multi-word groupings allows the modeling to differentiate a meaning-ful push statement, such as *Sq/CC next,* from the mere presence of the common terms *Sq/CC* and *next.*[1] We explored models that included groups of up to three words.

The matrix of documents by words and word groupings is called the *term-document matrix.* After constructing the term-document matrix, the next step is to populate the matrix with some measure of occurrence of the terms in each document. Measures of occurrence can include the simple presence or absence of a term or its raw count of occurrence. For short documents, such as an individual tweet on Twitter, presence or absence data might be sufficient. For longer docu-ments with more words, such as a collection of many officer perfor-mance narratives over several years, the most common frequency mea-sure is the *term frequency–inverse document frequency* (TFIDF).[2] The TFIDF metric combines two aspects of a term's occurrence. The first aspect, known as *term frequency,* measures how often the term appears

---

[1]   As discussed further in Chapter Five, in a *push statement,* raters can "push" officers for future positions, developmental opportunities, or leadership roles, and these statements carry significant weight because they imply the rater's assessment of the officer's potential.

[2]   A basic formula for TFIDF is as follows: For a given term, t, and document, d,

$$TFIDF_{t,d} = f_{t,d} * \log\frac{N}{n_t},$$

where $f_{t,d}$ is the number of times the term appears in the document (the term frequency), N is the total number of documents, and n_t is the number of documents containing the term (and the logarithm of N divided by n_t is the inverse document frequency).

in the current record. The second aspect, *inverse document frequency*, measures how common the term is across all records in the data set.

By combining these two key facets of each term, TFIDF provides a signal for which terms might be most informative to the ML algorithm. Intuitively, TFIDF assigns more importance to a word that frequently occurs in a single document but is rare across the whole set of documents. Conversely, TFIDF down-weights even the frequent occurrence of a term in a particular document if that term is common across the whole set of documents. For example, within the officer OPRs, common action words, such as *led* or *organized*, would receive low values for TFIDF, informing the system that they are less meaningful than are rare terms reserved for top performers (such as the previously referenced push statements recommending the officer for command, school, or high-level staff positions).

Processing the raw text into the form of a TFIDF matrix makes it easier for the ML algorithms to mimic the process by which a human judge would score the records. For terms that are not important for communicating performance, the TFIDF values would not relate strongly to the labels. For terms that do indicate good performance, the ML algorithms would discover an association between officers with higher TFIDF values for those terms and the labels indicating the best performance narratives. Then, for officers that accumulate important terms over the course of their annual evaluations, the AI system would produce higher levels of its performance metric output.

A suitably trained ML model can then predict the performance level of a narrative for officers at any point in their careers. It is important to note that generating the performance metric requires that the new narrative data be supplied as inputs in exactly the format and structure supplied to the initial ML algorithm. For new predictions, the analyst would proceed through the same formatting steps but using narratives for which the indicated performance level is unknown. The trained model can then use the relationships it has learned to predict the officer performance level for the new set of records.

Example of Processing Applied to Officer Performance Narratives

Figure 4.1 illustrates a simplified example of the data processing steps as applied to officer performance narratives. The figure begins with some notional performance narratives in the typical writing style of OPR bullets. OPR bullets are highly symbolic, and they contain mostly word fragments or abbreviations squished into a single line with very limited syntax. The narrative for Officer A contains several positive performance indicators readily apparent to a human judge: The officer won a wing-level annual award ("Wg CGOY"), was the top officer in his or her grade tier ("#1 of 103 CGOs"), and was recommended for a key developmental opportunity ("must for in res PME"[3]). By contrast, Officer B's narrative is vague and generic, which, in Air Force writing, tends to be an indicator of below-average performance.

The first processing step creates the term-document matrix by translating the words in the narratives into a matrix that indicates the presence of each word (stripped of punctuation and capitalization) and the number of times it appears in each narrative. At this stage, the structure of the bullets and word order are lost (for this reason, the method is sometimes referred to as a *bag-of-words approach*). The second processing step converts the word counts into TFIDF, which adjusts for how common the word is across all narratives. Thus, rare but meaningful terms, such as *cgoy* and *#1* receive higher TFIDF values, while more-common terms, such as *cgo* and *all*, receive lower TFIDF values. The step of going from raw word counts to TFIDF is not required, but it tends to help in the modeling phase by highlighting words that are likely to be more meaningful to the ML algorithm. Finally, the ML model uses the values in the TFIDF matrix in conjunction with the labels (i.e., selected for promotion versus not selected) to learn which key terms are most strongly associated with a narrative's indication of performance quality. In the example, it is likely that the signals in Officer A's narrative will strongly relate to promotion, so the AI system will

---

[3]   In the Air Force, top performers are selected to attend professional military education in residence (i.e., "in res").

Figure 4.1
Example Data Preparation Steps for Officer Performance Narratives

Performance narratives

Officer A: Wg CGOY... #1 of 103 CGOs--must for in res PME
Officer B: Good CGO; perf'd all duties--good in job!

Term-document matrix

	wg	cgoy	#1	of	103	cgos	must	for	in	res	pme	good	cgo	perfd	all	duties	job
ID1	1	1	1	1	1	1	1	1	1	1	1	0	0	0	0	0	0
ID2	0	0	0	0	0	0	0	0	1	0	0	2	1	1	1	1	1

TFIDF matrix

	wg	cgoy	#1	of	103	cgos	must	for	in	res	pme	good	cgo	perfd	all	duties	job
ID1	0.03	0.5	0.6	0.001	0.03	0.01	0.01	0.001	0.001	0.20	0.30	0	0	0	0	0	0
ID2	0	0	0	0	0	0	0	0	0.001	0.20	0	0.02	0.01	0.20	0.001	0.01	0.01

ML model

Finds associations between word combinations and outcome labels

NOTE: CGO = company-grade officer; PME = professional military education; Wg CGOY = Wing Company-Grade Officer of the Year.

use these relationships to infer that future officers whose narratives describe the same awards or peer rankings deserve a higher value for the predicted performance level.

Potential Refinements for Improving Future Models

The bag-of-words approach is a logical starting point in this application of AI, given that officer performance narratives communicate information by squeezing word fragments together on a single line and not through syntactic relationships between words. This approach also minimizes the labor required to develop and maintain the system by largely automating the data processing steps. The primary drawback of a bag-of-words approach is that it ignores the underlying meaning of the words and the semantic relationships between them. For instance, the example in Figure 4.1 shows that the approach considers *cgoy*, *cgos*, and *cgo* to be distinct words even though they contain the same root abbreviation for company-grade officer. Furthermore, the word *in* receives a low weight in the TFIDF calculation because it is a common word, but a human judge knows that the combination of *in* and *res* has important meaning for performance because officers compete based on performance to attend developmental education in residence. In this application, we attempt to mitigate for the latter shortfall by allowing groups of words (bigrams and trigrams), which means that the phrase *in res pme* could be considered a standalone word, along with the phrase *#1 of 103*. And the flexibility in the modeling phase allows for the consideration of a variety of complex relationships between words, as we describe in the next chapter. Although ML algorithms have no understanding of the content of words, they can often still accurately approximate human decisions using only TFIDF values for individual words.

Applying richer techniques that can use the contextual relationships between words in the written context would be a logical next step to explore in future work (Gentzkow, Kelly, and Taddy, 2019). Analysts can then judge the value of these techniques by the degree to which they improve the model's performance over the baseline bag-of-words method.

CHAPTER FIVE

Modeling the Relationship Between Performance Narratives and Promotion

Modeling Roadmap

- We applied two ML approaches—support vector machines (SVMs) and artificial neural networks (ANNs)—to the problem of using processed officer performance narratives to predict the likelihood of an officer being selected for promotion to an O-5 or O-6 position.
- The ML models were successful at linking patterns in the narratives to promotion outcomes, yielding a system that can calculate a performance index from any set of narratives.
- Analysis of the model outputs points to stratifications and push statements as key sources for information underlying the performance index, which accords with the foundational principles and guidance for writing Air Force performance reviews.

Modeling Approaches for Linking Processed Performance Narratives to Promotion Outcomes

In the data understanding and data preparation phases, we obtained and processed the officer performance narratives and linked them to quality labels from promotion board results. To execute the modeling phase of the CRISP-DM, we explored two very common ML approaches and observed their performance. In this chapter, we describe the process of exploring the modeling options to assess which might be most promising for further development.

We considered several ML approaches for the task of predicting promotion results based on the information in the processed performance narratives (i.e., the TFIDF matrix). These approaches include logistic regression, random forests, k-nearest neighbors algorithms, SVMs, and ANNs (Venables and Ripley, 2002). Existing research suggests that ANNs can address the most-complex pattern recognition challenges and often achieve the highest levels of performance (Javidi and Roshan, 2013; Zaydman, 2017). However, ANNs can require a large amount of input data before performance gains materialize. They can also be computationally expensive and difficult to interpret. Other algorithms can sometimes work suitably well when data are fewer, computational resources are more limited, or more-straightforward interpretation of model parameters is desired.

Particularly for textual data, SVMs often perform as a close second to ANNs in terms of predictive accuracy (Joachims, 1998). They also take much less effort to train. Whereas ANNs require the analyst to make several parameter tuning decisions, mostly with little theory to guide those decisions, SVMs require tuning only one or two parameters that assign costs for how many variable interactions are allowed in the model. For this exploratory assessment, then, we chose to examine the performance of SVMs and ANNs.

Model Validation

ML algorithms learn to predict the labeled training data within some prespecified structure that constrains how variables are combined and interacted in the model. This presents a risk of the model *overfitting*, which occurs when a model has fit the patterns in the training data too closely, and, therefore, the model will not perform well on new data. ML models, in particular, are prone to overfitting because they can include many possible variables in a model that is allowed to grow to be extremely complex (Domingos, 2012).

To avoid overfitting, data scientists examine model performance by earmarking subsets of the data to be intentionally excluded from the training process. Seeing how well the model predicts results for this hold-out subset of data that has been isolated for testing provides information on how the model will perform on new data in the future. There is an additional risk that, even if the ML model has not seen the testing data in the fitting process, repeatedly using the testing data to inform the model calibration can also lead to a type of overfitting. Thus, analysts typically use one hold-out data set for tuning the models (known as validation data) in addition to the testing data (Chollet and Allaire, 2018). In this analysis, we selected a 20-percent random sample of data for testing and then used a 20-percent sample of the remaining data for validation.[1] The final performance statistics that we describe in this chapter rely on the test data, which were entirely new to the ML model at the time of performance testing.

Modeling Results

Similar Levels of Performance for Both Approaches

Table 5.1 shows a comparison of the SVM and ANN algorithms using three performance metrics: accuracy, precision, and recall. These results rely solely on the TFIDF method of processing the officer per-

Table 5.1
Model Results

Sample	Model	Base Rate of Selection	Accuracy	Precision	Recall
O-5	SVM	0.766	0.822	0.855	0.924
O-5	ANN	0.766	0.818	0.827	0.965
O-6	SVM	0.482	0.750	0.747	0.729
O-6	ANN	0.482	0.747	0.754	0.706

---

[1]   Another option to guard against overfitting without losing data to the hold-out sets is to use cross-validation. This technique involves splitting the data into equal groups and repeatedly fitting the model to all but one of the groups while using the remaining group as a hold-out set. The predictive performance for each observation in the data when it was part of the rotating hold-out set is the proxy for the model's predictive accuracy on new data.

formance narratives using unigrams, bigrams, and trigrams.[2] For ease of computation, we restricted the input terms to those that appeared in a minimum number of officer records (100 for O-6 and 200 for O-5).

Each of the three performance metrics provides a window into how well the models differentiate the highest-quality records (i.e., officers selected for promotion) from the lower-quality records. To calculate the metrics, we predicted whether each record in the test data would be selected based solely on whether the ML model gave the record at least a 50-percent chance of selection. Accuracy captures the overall tendency for the model to correctly predict whether an officer was selected for promotion. Precision is the percentage of predicted selections that were actually selected for promotion, which captures the tendency for the model to yield false positives. Recall captures the coverage of the predicted selections and is calculated as the percentage of all actual selections that the ML model predicted. Precision and recall, when viewed together, illustrate the reality that encouraging a model to correctly identify more of the officers who were ultimately selected (higher recall) might thereby increase the risk of generating false positives (lower precision).

Any accuracy metric must further be interpreted in the context of the base rate of selection, which Table 5.1 also lists for each model. Higher values of the three metrics indicate better model performance, but the base rate further serves as a predictive benchmark. A naïve model that predicts that all officers will be selected will have an accuracy level equal to the base rate of selection. Thus, the base rate is a starting point for the level of accuracy. Furthermore, randomly choosing a group of predicted selections that is the same size as the base rate would have precision and recall values equal to the base rate of selection, so it is also a useful benchmark for these values.

All four models show improved predictive performance over the base rate of selection, and the SVM and ANN algorithms perform

---

[2]   We also performed some initial exploration of incorporating how the terms appear in context, an approach known as *word embeddings*. These techniques go beyond the bag-of-words approach in order to capture relationships between words. The models that tested word embeddings performed similarly to the bag-of-words models shown in Table 5.1.

similarly with some variation in precision and recall. The relative improvement over the base rate is greatest in the O-6 models; there is roughly a 50-percent improvement in accuracy for the O-6 models compared with a 6-percent improvement for the O-5 models. The limited improvement for the O-5 models highlights the potential benefit of using the richer order-of-merit information for labels instead of using the final promotion outcome. When the base rate of selection is very high, this limits the ability of the ML algorithm to differentiate performance quality among the narratives.

Preserving Relative Performance Rankings When Considering Partial Records

In our discussion of the data understanding phase, we noted that one potential drawback of using promotion results as quality labels is that the expert assessment of records for promotion to O-5 and O-6 positions takes place late in an officer's career. This raises the question of whether the resulting AI system would be immediately useful to assess performance among officers at earlier career points. Examining this question directly would require knowledge of the relative performance of officers at different points in their careers, which is not available. However, to indirectly assess this question, we compared the predicted performance index for officers up to five years before each promotion board with the predicted index for officers at the time of the board. This exercise will not perfectly measure whether the performance index accurately reflects the true performance level at these earlier points because it implausibly assumes that the final index is the true level of performance and there is no variation in relative performance over time. However, it is still useful to assess whether there is some stability in the performance index when it is based on an incomplete record of performance narratives.

Tables 5.2 and 5.3 show the percentage of officers that remain in the same percentile group as they would be with full information for various time points prior to the promotion board. (Note that the remaining tables and figures in this chapter are based on the ANN model only.) The columns in Tables 5.2 and 5.3 show different levels of percentile granularity. For instance, the left-most value in the first

Table 5.2
Percentage of O-5 Candidates Who Remain in the Same Percentile Group over Time

Time to Promotion Board	Percentile Group Width			
	5 Percentage Points (%)	10 Percentage Points (%)	20 Percentage Points (%)	25 Percentage Points (%)
1 year prior	36.9	57.2	77.9	82.4
2 years prior	29.8	45.6	69.5	73.3
3 years prior	23.0	38.0	62.1	66.9
4 years prior	19.5	32.5	55.0	60.4
5 years prior	16.7	28.6	47.5	54.3

Table 5.3
Percentage of O-6 Candidates Who Remain in the Same Percentile Group over Time

Time to Promotion Board	Percentile Group Width			
	5 Percentage Points (%)	10 Percentage Points (%)	20 Percentage Points (%)	25 Percentage Points (%)
1 year prior	29.7	49.9	73.7	78.0
2 years prior	24.5	38.5	64.6	71.7
3 years prior	19.7	31.5	55.9	64.6
4 years prior	17.3	30.4	51.1	60.4
5 years prior	14.9	26.4	49.2	59.2

row of Table 5.2 means that, if we assign each officer to a percentile grouping that is 5 percentage points wide, 36.9 percent of the officers would remain in the same grouping when using the performance index that is based on records that closed out one year prior to the O-5 promotion board.

While all officers will tend to have lower performance indices when the ML model evaluates only a portion of their records, these results show that there is some consistency in the relative ranking of the performance index, even when calculated for officers up to five years prior to each promotion board.[3] If an HR process needed a quantitative performance input for officers between the O-4 and O-5 promotion milestones, for instance, the predicted index from the O-5 model would correctly match 50–80 percent of the officers to the quintile or quartile that they might ultimately attain at the time of the next promotion board. This consistency stems from the fact that the ML model has identified a set of phrases that are strongly related to future board decisions, so the presence of some of those terms in a partial record can still help an AI system understand an individual's level of performance relative to other officers at the same career point.

Terms That Most Strongly Relate to the Performance Index

The flexibility of ML algorithms, such as SVMs and ANNs, allows them to capture rich and complex relationships between the text in a performance narrative and fine gradations in performance. A potential downside, which we discuss further in Chapter Six, is that it becomes difficult to discern which aspects of the text have the strongest influence on the performance output. Many high-performing ML algorithms do not lend themselves naturally to metrics that associate the inputs (text fragments, in our case) with the outcome.

One workaround to gain some understanding of an ML model is to analyze the model's outputs with more-transparent statistical methods. In Figures 5.1 and 5.2, we display 30 of the top terms (the top ten in each category) that are most positively correlated with predicted quality; Figure 5.1 shows results based on the O-5 model, and Figure 5.2 shows results based on the O-6 model. In each ML model, the predicted quality draws on thousands of possible terms and combinations of terms, but the fact that these terms are strongly correlated with the model output suggests that they have high importance in the underlying model.

---

[3] This roughly translates to the time of the prior grade's promotion board, when the officers' records would receive a full manual evaluation.

Figure 5.1
Top Terms That Most Highly Correlate with the Performance Index from O-5 Outcomes

Unigrams (0.19, 0.31)*	Bigrams (0.15, 0.25)*	Trigrams (0.11, 0.15)*
1	sq_cc	sq_cc_1
cgos	1_of	then_jt_staff
cc	jt_staff	top_1_of
1st	my_1	i_ve_seen
yr	o_4s	ops_sq_cc
4	cc_1	ve_seen_in
jt	1_4	absolute_must_for
yrs	cgos_in	rater_is_also
2	must_for	must_for_ide
ldr	1_3	is_also_the

NOTE: * indicates the range of correlations. The font size of the terms is proportional to the correlation, and the terms in each category are in descending order from largest to smallest.

Overall, the figures provide a window into how the data processing in an ML approach differs from how a human might read and interpret the same narratives. An AI system mimics human judgment by breaking each officer's performance narratives into fragments and using the promotion outcomes to infer which combinations of fragments are apparently important to the human judges. Thus, the text fragments in Figures 5.1 and 5.2 have inklings of meaning, but none is individually meaningful apart from the ML model's prediction process.

This simple exercise provides a layer of face validity to the approach by showing that the ML algorithm has detected fragments of information that an experienced judge would look for. Nearly all of the terms in Figures 5.1 and 5.2 likely relate to the following two categories

Figure 5.2
Top Terms That Most Highly Correlate with the Performance Index from O-6 Outcomes

Unigrams (0.25, 0.35)*	Bigrams (0.23, 0.43)*	Trigrams (0.16, 0.23)*
ccs	sq_ccs	then_jt_staff
jt	jt_staff	then_og_cc
amn	cc_1	jt_staff_then
1	gp_cc	6_sq_ccs
cc	1_6	gp_cc_1
awd	then_jt	then_msg_cc
awds	cc_led	then_joint_staff
1st	og_cc	og_cc_1
13	msg_cc	cgo_of_the
4	5_sq	joint_staff_1

NOTE: * indicates the range of correlations. The font size of the terms is proportional to the correlation, and the terms in each category are in descending order from largest to smallest.

of information that are foundational to writing Air Force performance reviews (U.S. Air Force Reserve, undated):

- *Stratifications:* Raters can provide a "quantitative comparison of an individual standing among peers" within a system of rules and limitations. Officer records that contain consistent stratification through their performance narratives are more competitive for promotion.
- *Push statements:* Raters can "push" officers for future positions, developmental opportunities, or leadership roles, and these statements carry significant weight because they imply the rater's assessment of the officer's potential. The three main categories of

push statements include pushes for future positions (such as staff jobs), pushes for developmental education, and pushes for command positions.

The results in all three categories of both figures show that the ML model associates fragments of stratifications with higher performance. The top unigram from the O-5 model and the fourth unigram from the O-6 model are simply the number *1*, which is most likely to appear in the form of a stratification (e.g., *#1/100 CGOs*). Related terms, such as *1_3* and *top_1_of*, are also likely to be stratification fragments that the ML model identified as important in discriminating quality in both models.[4]

In addition to identifying stratifications, the results in Figures 5.1 and 5.2 clearly indicate that the ML model identified elements of push statements as closely related to officer performance quality indicated in the narratives. The phrases *must_for*, *absolute_must_for*, and *must_for_ide* are variations of these statements in which raters make recommendations for key assignments or positions. Furthermore, the ML model likely detected a relationship between the performance quality indicated and the push statements for the appropriate next level of command (*sq*, or squadron level, for the O-5 results, and *gp*, or group level, for the O-6 results). Finally, there is a hierarchy for pushes to staff positions; that is, recommending officers to higher echelons of staff suggests higher levels of officer performance and potential.[5] Without any awareness of this hierarchy, the ML algorithm keyed in on pushes for high-level joint staff (*jt_staff*) as an important indicator of performance quality.

In addition to identifying stratifications and push statements, the terms in Figures 5.1 and 5.2 identify other interesting attributes

---

[4]   Based on a priori knowledge of performance review writing, we initially explored models that explicitly stripped stratifications from the officer records and encoded those stratifications as a variable for the model. Specifically coding stratifications did not improve the performance of the ML models, and these results illustrate the reason why: The ML models were able to account for stratifications from the TFIDF matrix without explicit coding.

[5]   The hierarchy, descending order, is Air Force, major command, Headquarters Air Force, combatant command or joint, and Joint Chiefs of Staff or Office of the Secretary of Defense.

of narratives that indicate higher performance. For instance, several terms in the O-6 results indicate awards (*awd*, *awds*, and *cgo_of_the*). Furthermore, there is a logical explanation for the importance of the terms *rater_is_also* and *is_also_the*. Air Force rules stipulate that only one general officer can sign an evaluation. When officers work directly for general officers, the performance narrative will contain only one evaluation from the rater, while the additional rater block will contain the phrase "rater is also the additional rater" (Department of the Air Force, 2020a). Although this phrase is less important than other terms in the figure, the fact that the O-5 results identified fragments of this statement with higher-quality officer performance is telling: It suggests that the ratings of senior officers carry additional weight, all else being equal.

Illustration of Using the Model to Score Officer Performance Quality Based on Narratives

The key capability of the AI system built around an ML model is the ability to translate textual narratives directly into a performance index that HR managers could use either to augment their understanding of the performance information in a single record or to understand the performance distribution for a large group of officers. To illustrate this capability, we selected the record of one officer from the O-5 and O-6 samples who was not promoted in the primary zone. The performance index (on the same scale as the probability of being selected for promotion) for each record was roughly 0.25. This value indicates that the quality of each record is significantly below average. Boards selected roughly three in four officers in the O-5 sample and one in two officers in the O-6 sample, but only one in four narratives similar to those test cases would result in selection at each level.

We present these results in Figure 5.3. Each point in the figure moving from left to right shows what would happen if the selected officers received one or more additional OPRs with narratives that contain the terms in Figures 5.1 and 5.2. Adding half of the key terms in the figures (selected at random) boosts the performance index for each officer, but it is not until all the key terms are added to the record that each officer's performance begins to look like the average record for

Figure 5.3
Change in Performance Index Associated with Adjusted Performance Narrative Inputs

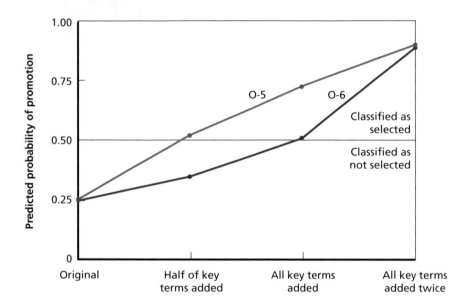

both samples. Continuing to add to the narratives until all key terms appear twice further boosts the performance index, especially for the O-6 model.

These results demonstrate a proof of concept for the proposed system. With no explicit rules, the NLP approaches described in this report successfully linked the information contained in officer performance narratives to expert judgments of the performance information. HR practitioners could then use this linkage to quantify the performance information in new records that no expert panel has formally evaluated. Furthermore, depending on the desired use of the system, other data sources or new data collection techniques could improve the system and overcome the previously discussed shortcomings of this baseline model that has been trained to mimic O-5 and O-6 promotion board decisions.

CHAPTER SIX

Evaluating Other Implementation Considerations

Evaluation Roadmap

- Using an AI performance-scoring system for HRM requires that policymakers consider issues related to privacy, fairness, explainability, and other unintended consequences for personnel management.
- The degree to which these considerations present a barrier to implementation depends on how HRM processes use the AI system and the impact of the system on individual careers.
- These considerations raise issues for each potential use of the proposed system, but concerns are greatest if the system were used to make decisions that would alter officers' careers.
- These considerations could be less of a barrier to implementing the system as a tool to facilitate policy analysis or to assist development teams, and the considerations would not present a concern if the system were merely used as a teaching tool for professional development.

Privacy

AI analytics have fundamentally different privacy concerns compared with conventional analytics. A conventional analysis usually begins with a selection of factors based on a theoretical or conceptual framework. Then, an analyst develops models to capture associations among the selected factors. In contrast, the AI analysis identifies factors and uncovers their associations by applying the ML techniques to data that are rich in content and expansive in scope. As a result, the potential for breaching privacy is higher in AI analysis than in conventional analysis, even when analysts take care to remove personally identifiable information from the data. Therefore, the AI system must include safeguards against violations of privacy (Kelleher and Tierney, 2018).

The privacy considerations in the proposed applications stem from the sensitivity of individual records of job performance. In current practice, access to these records is limited to the officers whose records are under consideration and to others who need to access those records in an official capacity (such as supervisors or HR managers). The AI applications that associate a performance metric with an individual, which include an application's use by development teams and for selection decisions, would likely carry the same level of sensitivity. Data for policy analysis, by contrast, could be de-identified and would likely carry no additional privacy risk compared with other individual-level information stored in personnel data systems. Finally, the AI system would not need to retain individual-level performance information, so the privacy risk of using the system as a teaching tool would be minimal.

Fairness

HR decisions must provide equal opportunities to all members of the organization, regardless of their background characteristics. For instance, DoD policy maintains the Military Equal Opportunity Program to ensure that all DoD personnel are afforded an environment free from "unlawful discrimination on the basis of race, color, national origin, religion, sex (including gender identity), or sexual orientation" (DoD, 2018b, p. 6). The law generally prohibits both intentional or overt discrimination and protects employees against the disparate impact of a seemingly neutral practice that negatively affects some people in a protected class more than others. In addition, using an AI system in an Air Force HRM context requires that personnel in a wide variety of employment contexts (such as different mission areas and career fields) perceive that it is fair and unbiased.

Ensuring fairness when using a complex algorithm in HRM decisions requires more than omitting sensitive attributes, such as protected class membership, from the model. ML models are adept at discovering proxies for these characteristics even if they are not explicit in the data (Osoba et al., 2019). The primary application in which fairness would be a chief concern, then, is the use of an AI system to inform competitive selection decisions. Even if an AI-assisted performance-scoring system is intentionally denied information on each officer's protected statuses, such as gender and race, there is a risk that AI techniques are flexible enough to infer the statuses using combinations of other variables. Hence, the AI system could integrate any historical (intentional or unintentional) biases into its performance scores.

For example, minority officers in the Air Force might be more likely to serve in recruiting assignments involving outreach activities to minority communities. As a result, the OPRs of minority officers would contain references to those activities. If minority officers, historically, were less likely to be selected for career advancement or developmental education opportunities, the AI system might use engaging in outreach activities (a proxy for race) as a negative factor in scoring officer performance. Unless Air Force leaders intentionally consider those activities undesirable, the developer of the system needs to be vigilant and build safeguards against such instances, such as testing procedures for repairing training data to make ML algorithms less likely to produce a discriminatory result (Adjunwa et al., 2016).

At the same time, two mitigating factors apply to this application. First, prior research on the Air Force promotion system has found similar promotion outcomes regardless of race/ethnicity and gender, once differences in other characteristics are considered (Lim et al., 2014). Second, unlike typical big-data applications that take a wide variety of personal information as potential inputs, this system considers information from officer performance narratives only. The information included in these narratives is tightly regulated and is explicitly for the purpose of documenting performance for HRM. Thus, if policymakers and individuals perceive promotion boards (or an alternative process of generating outcome labels) as fair, then an AI system that faithfully replicates the labels and does not systematically err in favor of particular groups might also be acceptable.

A final consideration regarding general fairness involves the acceptable level of model error. As shown in the previous chapter, the model evaluations differ from expert judgments, such as promotion board decisions, a certain percentage of the time. If performance metrics from an AI system were included in competitive selection decisions, it could be unfair to service members who are scored lower by the AI system than they would be by a board of experts (although standardized metrics could benefit other members who might have scored lower as a result of human error in a board process). One option to address this concern would be to use the AI system to select records for review by human judges rather than to make the ultimate selection decision. The selection process could also incorporate randomization, which employees are more likely to perceive as fair (Tambe, Cappelli, and Yakubovich, 2019), by including a random sample of records from across the performance quality spectrum (with a greater likelihood of inclusion for individuals with higher performance indices). These randomly selected records have the added benefit of serving as additional training examples that are useful in refining the AI system (see Chapter Three).

Explainability

The power of ML algorithms is their flexibility to capture underlying associations in the data without imposing a rigid structure (Alpaydin, 2016). This also means that the resulting models are difficult to summarize and explain (Kelleher and Tierney, 2018), although more-explainable techniques are an active area of research for DoD initiatives, such as the Explainable AI program at the Defense Advanced Research Projects Agency. Hence, so-called black-box models lack transparency, which is a cornerstone of effective HR policies and practices. Widespread buy-in for the adoption of an AI system in HRM requires that employees who are affected by the system understand the way that attributes are factored into decisions. To take a non-HR example, prior research in the field of medicine shows that both doctors and patients have difficulty accepting diagnoses from AI systems because of the difficulty with understanding how the algorithm produced its recommendation (Tambe, Cappelli, and Yakubovich, 2019).

Explainability is generally a limiting factor of the system described in this report in its current form for all of the potential applications, as each would benefit from a better understanding of the underlying attributes that determine the predictions. The degree to which explainability limits implementation is the highest for use in selection, which could include such high-stakes decisions as key developmental opportunities. For the other applications, the lack of explainability could affect the usefulness of the AI system, but it might be less of a barrier to implementation.

Unintended Consequences of Implementation

As we discussed earlier, typical applications of AI to HRM tend to be backward-looking in that they draw heavily on the historical definitions of good performance. Depending on the HRM function of the AI system, this tendency could harm HRM policy in the long run. An example of this pitfall is the naïve application of ML models to identify the most-promising job candidates for hiring based on the attributes of historical top performers. Using such a model to screen new hires could cause HR managers to focus on new hires that resemble those successful in the past while overlooking promising candidates with different or novel backgrounds. If managers never hire anyone with a different background from that of the historically successful employees, they would never know that this was a problem because they would never see the performance of the candidates who were never hired.

Implementing an AI system for selection decisions carries a similar risk of unintended consequences, because selection for competitive opportunities (such as developmental assignments) affects subsequent performance. Selecting officers who are recommended by the AI system and who have attributes that match historical top performers would cause those officers to appear to become top performers themselves, by virtue of the opportunities they receive (a sort of self-fulfilling prophecy). This problem is not necessarily unique to AI and likely exists in some form as part of current practices. However, an AI-assisted system that increases the reach of these historical performance-scoring practices could make the problem worse. Policymakers should therefore carefully consider how the AI-based performance metrics interact with other developmental and advancement policies.

Conclusion and Policy Implications

Having explored each step in the CRISP-DM framework for the problem of creating an AI-enabled performance-scoring system to use in Air Force HRM processes, we now revisit the framework to discuss the feasibility of the system at each step. In this chapter, we also provide more strategic policy implications for decisionmakers to consider for future AI applications in HRM.

Artificial Intelligence Performance-Scoring System Exploratory Assessment

Figure 7.1 displays the steps in the CRISP-DM framework alongside the inputs and outputs associated with the AI application discussed in this report. The figure provides a helpful summary of the path that Air Force analysts would take to go from the information in OES databases to a fully functional capability that HR managers could use to assist in decisionmaking. Once HR managers validate a business need, they would pull a set of officer evaluation records from the databases and digitize them so that the performance narratives and other text would be available for analysis. Then, analysts would process those narratives in a variety of ways so that they could be input into a model that predicts performance from the text. Given the model and desired application, HR managers could then evaluate the considerations discussed in the previous chapter to arrive at an implementation plan before finally standing up an information technology infrastructure that allows users to incorporate the model into HRM processes.

Figure 7.1
Exploratory Assessment of the Artificial Intelligence Performance-Scoring System

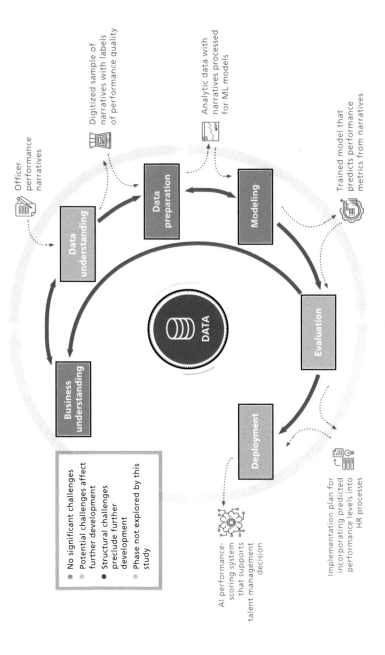

Using our experience from the current worked example, we assigned colors to the boxes for each step to highlight the areas where the Air Force could face challenges with further development or implementation. Figure 7.1 includes no red boxes (which would indicate structural challenges that preclude system development), given that results in the previous chapters demonstrate that some version of this system is feasible. Figure 7.1 shows the business understanding, data preparation, and modeling phases in green because we did not encounter any significant challenges in these areas. We were able to establish a preliminary business need for the AI performance-scoring system, and once we successfully digitized the OES data, the steps involved in processing the text and building a model to predict performance levels were straightforward. The figure shows the data understanding phase in yellow to highlight the potential challenge to future efforts of accurately extracting enough OPR text from historical records, because they currently include only images of the OPR forms in a variety of formats. The figure also flags the evaluation phase in yellow to highlight the potential challenges of using the system in certain applications, such as high-stakes selection decisions that affect individual careers. Finally, the deployment phase is shown in gray to reflect the fact that we did not explore the details of designing an infrastructure that could host the system once HR managers had decided on implementation.

Policy Implications

For this study, we focused on an example with an intentionally narrow scope. However, the process of investigating this application highlighted three strategic considerations for HRM policymakers to consider going forward.

Policymakers Should Position Systems and Policies to Take Advantage of Analytic Uses of Data That HRM Processes Generate

OPRs represent a living repository of information on the duties of each officer and his or her accomplishments. These data are rich in detail, especially compared with the auxiliary information that the personnel and manpower data systems capture about individuals and positions. These other data systems mainly capture high-level categories of information (such as duty titles, occupation codes, required grade levels, and unit designators) that were designed to *limit* detail for efficiency. Without the OES data, HR managers know very little about what each officer is actually doing or how job responsibilities and activities might be changing over time.

Because current processes were designed prior to the advent of modern analytic techniques, they inhibit the use of this rich information for general analytic purposes outside of performance management. For instance, current processes do not archive OES records in a way that is easily accessible to HR analysts. Furthermore, current policies prevent promotion board scores from being used outside of the boards themselves, despite the possible usefulness of this information for performance analysis. These two examples highlight the general need for a different paradigm that positions future systems and policies to take advantage of the analytic uses of information stored in the personnel system beyond the specific HR process that generates it.

Natural Language Processing Techniques Can Reduce the Need to Pre-Quantify Information at the Data Collection Stage

This analysis also highlights a potential paradigm shift in the way HR managers use textual data. Typical data collection instruments in HRM and elsewhere include a combination of numeric or categorical ratings and unstructured text. The categorical ratings are readily amenable to statistical analysis, while the text offers respondents the opportunity to elaborate on aspects of the topic that the numeric or categorical questions might not capture. Under the pre-NLP paradigm, analysts would summarize the numeric and categorical information statistically while manually reviewing a subset of the comments for additional insights. Textual information had the significant downside of being difficult to process and summarize systematically.

The current example shows that NLP techniques for analyzing textual data have reduced this downside by making it possible to automate aspects of the manual processing. Under the old paradigm, a statistical summary of OPRs (which are 100-percent text under current policy) would require a process of manual review and scoring. This analysis shows that NLP can allow statistical analyses to incorporate textual information as *data*, alongside numeric inputs, to support decisionmaking. Thus, when collecting information for HRM decisions, planners could be more open to collecting unstructured text if warranted, because this information can be folded directly into statistical analyses. For example, as the Air Force considers incorporating numeric rating scales into officer evaluations (Losey, 2019), policymakers should consider that the benefits of performance narratives, as a richer medium for performance feedback (Brutus, 2010), no longer come with the drawback of being difficult to quantify for HRM processes that compare performance across individuals.

Policymakers Should Consider Artificial Intelligence to Be an Enabler of Better Policies Rather Than a Substitute for Human Decisionmaking

Finally, our analysis at the evaluation stage of this application highlights that using an AI system to make HRM decisions, such as in a competitive selection context, would place a high burden of proof on HR managers to demonstrate that the AI system is fair, is explainable, and minimizes the risk of unintended consequences. This assessment is consistent with known AI adoption challenges in the civilian sector. However, the alternative uses of the AI system to support policy analysis, professional development, or training likely carry a lower risk of harm and could be more readily adopted. The common thread in these alternative uses is that they incorporate the AI system as an enabler of better HRM policies without substituting for human judgment and decisionmaking. Although technological progress could improve the prospects of crafting an AI system that is free of bias and easier to explain to affected personnel, there could be greater promise in the near term for applications that enable improved HRM policy than for applications that rely on AI systems to make consequential personnel decisions.

Conclusion

As policymakers continue to emphasize AI adoption to make processes more efficient and effective, this application illustrates the possibilities and challenges associated with adoption efforts. Existing data collection procedures born from a different set of business needs might not be optimal for use in analytics. Furthermore, policymakers will need to wrestle with each application to answer not just whether they *can* use AI to perform a task but also whether they *should*. This study illustrates how Air Force analysts can approach these problems systematically, as well as some larger directions that HRM policy in the Air Force can take to further encourage adoption of AI in HRM processes.

References

Adjunwa, Ifeoma, Sorelle Freidler, Carlos Scheidegger, and Suresh Venkatasubramanian, "Hiring by Algorithm: Predicting and Preventing Disparate Impact," *Data and Society*, March 10, 2016.

Aguinis, Herman, *Performance Management*, 3rd ed., Boston: Pearson Education, 2013.

Air Reserve Personnel Center, "Evaluations," webpage, undated. As of November 9, 2020:
https://www.arpc.afrc.af.mil/Services/Evaluations/

Alpaydin, Ethem, *Machine Learning*, Cambridge, Mass.: MIT Press, 2016.

Brutus, Stephane, "Words Versus Numbers: A Theoretical Exploration of Giving and Receiving Narrative Comments in Performance Appraisal," *Human Resource Management Review*, Vol. 20, No. 2, 2010, pp. 144–157.

Brynjolfsson, Erik, and Tom Mitchell, "What Can Machine Learning Do? Workforce Implications," *Science*, Vol. 358, No. 6370, 2017, pp. 1530–1534.

Chapman, Pete, Julian Clinton, Randy Kerber, Thomas Khabaza, Thomas Reinartz, Colin Shearer, and Rüdiger Wirth, *CRISP-DM 1.0: Step-by-Step Data Mining Guide*, NCR Systems Engineering Copenhagen, DaimlerChrysler AG, SPSS Inc., and OHRA Verzekeringen en Bank Groep B.V., 2000.

Chollet, François, and J. J. Allaire, *Deep Learning with R*, Shelter Island, N.Y.: Manning Publications, 2018.

Department of the Air Force, "Air Force Guidance Memorandum to AFI 36-2406, *Officer and Enlisted Evaluation Systems*," Washington, D.C., May 20, 2020a. As of November 9, 2020:
https://static.e-publishing.af.mil/production/1/af_a1/publication/afi36-2406/afi36-2406.pdf

———, "Air Force Guidance Memorandum (AFGM) to AFI 36-2670, *Total Force Development*," Washington, D.C., September 29, 2020b. As of November 9, 2020:
https://static.e-publishing.af.mil/production/1/af_a1/publication/afi36-2670/afi36-2670.pdf

DoD—*See* U.S. Department of Defense.

Domingos, Pedro, "A Few Useful Things to Know About Machine Learning," *Communications of the ACM*, Vol. 55, No. 10, October 2012, pp. 78–87.

Fountaine, Tim, Brian McCarthy, and Tamim Saleh, "Building the AI-Powered Organization," *Harvard Business Review*, July–August, 2019.

Gentzkow, Matthew, Bryan Kelly, and Matt Taddy, "Text as Data," *Journal of Economic Literature*, Vol. 57, No. 3, 2019, pp. 535–574.

Javidi, Mohammad Masoud, and Ebrahim Fazlizadeh Roshan, "Speech Emotion Recognition by Using Combinations of C5. 0, Neural Network (NN), and Support Vector Machines (SVM) Classification Methods," *Journal of Mathematics and Computer Science*, Vol. 6, 2013, pp. 191–200.

Joachims, Thorsten, "Text Categorization with Support Vector Machines: Learning with Many Relevant Features," ECML '98 Proceedings of the European Conference on Machine Learning, 1998, pp. 137–142.

Jordan, M. I., and T. M. Mitchell, "Machine Learning: Trends, Perspectives, and Prospects," *Science*, Vol. 349, No. 6245, 2015, pp. 255–260.

Kelleher, John D., and Brendan Tierney, *Data Science*, Cambridge, Mass.: MIT Press, 2018.

Lim, Nelson, Louis T. Mariano, Amy G. Cox, David Schulker, and Lawrence M. Hanser, *Improving Demographic Diversity in the U.S. Air Force Officer Corps*, Santa Monica, Calif.: RAND Corporation, RR-495-AF, 2014. As of November 17, 2020:
https://www.rand.org/pubs/research_reports/RR495.html

Losey, Stephen, "'Ned Stark' Takes the Stage at AFA; a Remarkably Candid Discussion of Leadership Ensues," *Air Force Times*, September 19, 2019.

Mariscal, Gonzalo, Oscar Marban, and Covadonga Fernandez, "A Survey of Data Mining and Knowledge Discovery Process Models and Methodologies," *Knowledge Engineering Review*, Vol. 25, No. 2, 2010, pp. 137–166.

Murphy, Robert F., *Artificial Intelligence Applications to Support K–12 Teachers and Teaching: A Review of Promising Applications, Challenges, and Risks*, Santa Monica, Calif.: RAND Corporation, PE-315-RC, 2019. As of June 2, 2020:
https://www.rand.org/pubs/perspectives/PE315.html

Osoba, Osonde A., Benjamin Boudreaux, Jessica Saunders, J. Luke Irwin, Pam A. Mueller, and Samantha Cherney, *Algorithmic Equity: A Framework for Social Applications*, Santa Monica, Calif.: RAND Corporation, RR-2708-RC, 2019. As of November 9, 2020:
https://www.rand.org/pubs/research_reports/RR2708.html

Tambe, Prasanna, Peter Cappelli, and Valery Yakubovich, "Artificial Intelligence in Human Resources Management: Challenges and a Path Forward," *California Management Review*, Vol. 61, No. 4, 2019, pp. 15–42.

Tierney, Winston S., "Words Have Meaning: Are You Aware of What You Are Writing?" *Marine Corps Gazette*, 2019.

U.S. Air Force Reserve, "Performance Evaluations," briefing slides, undated. As of November 9, 2020:
https://www.arpc.afrc.af.mil/Portals/4/DRIO/Training/IRO-augustSlides/RIO-IRO-Performance-Evaluations.pdf?ver=2018-09-13-115249-703

U.S. Department of Defense, *Summary of the 2018 Department of Defense Artificial Intelligence Strategy: Harnessing AI to Advance Our Security and Prosperity*, Washington, D.C., 2018a.

———, *Diversity Management and Equal Opportunity in the DoD*, Department of Defense Directive 1020.02E, Washington, D.C., June 1, 2018b.

Venables, William N., and Brian D. Ripley, *Modern Applied Statistics with S*, 4th ed., New York: Springer, 2002.

Wolfgeher, Stephane L., *Inflation of USAF Officer Performance Reports: Analyzing the Organizational Environment*, thesis, Monterey, Calif.: Naval Postgraduate School, 2009.

Zaydman, Mikhail, *Tweeting About Mental Health: Big Data Text Analysis of Twitter for Public Policy*, dissertation, Pardee RAND Graduate School, Santa Monica, Calif.: RAND Corporation, RGSD-391, 2017. As of November 17, 2020:
https://www.rand.org/pubs/rgs_dissertations/RGSD391.html

Zhang, Mo, "Contrasting Automated and Human Scoring of Essays," *R&D Connections*, No. 21, March 2013. As of September 2, 2020:
http://origin-www.ets.org/Media/Research/pdf/RD_Connections_21.pdf